Political Prison Proposals Poll Plan

Taxpayers Wish List

Reverend Mike Wanner

Copyright
Rev. Mike Wanner
October 6, 2018

Selected Images Used by License

"Prison Presents" Tab
"Healing Presents" Tab

http://www.AngelRaphaelSpeaks.com

Table of Contents

Copyright 2
1 - Why I am Writing This Book 5
2 - Disclaimer 6
3 - Taxpayer Wish List 7
4 - A Precise Declaration Ready to Go 8
5 - Where To Start 9
6 - Red Tape 11
7 - Refined Legislation Could Cut Costs 12
8 - "Sentencing" (Example) 14
9 - Alcoholic Program Concept 16
10 - Drug Addict Program Concept 17
11 - Mental Health Program Concept 18
12 - Recidivism 19
13 - Children Need Access to Their Parents 20
14 - What Would We Vote For? 21
15 - Political Action Plan 22
16 - Proposed Declaration – City_____ 24
17 - Wrap Up 25
18 - Thank You 26
19 - Don't Worry Ever 27
20 - Books Category Resources 28
21 - Angels Please Prayers 29
22 - Private Channeling 30
23 - Reverend Mike Wanner 31

Introduction

Some sources report that in America alone that there are more than 2.3 million people in jail.

I like most people was entirely oblivious to that fact. I started channeling Angel Raphael in 2013 and began releasing little message sets as they came through.

In message set 16 of the Angel Raphael Speaks Series there was a message

"I asked Mike to Step into Prison Energetically

I have asked Mike to get the address and location within a prison of a designated space so he can visit energetically and receive feedback for us. Whether he will have time, interest or opportunity to do this will be interesting to see. As he writes this, he is not thrilled with the idea. We are already consuming a lot of his time." ARS16

I had resisted that invitation to visit jail energetically until 2016.

1 - Why I am Writing This Book

The invitation that I referenced just above was finally embraced in 2016. So far, The Angel Raphael prodding has had me publish over sixty books about prison possibilities.

I focus on possibilities because the existing circumstances we find ourselves in are a progressive mess that is **NOT blamable** on any living being, so fault finding is a waste of time.

The old-time rule writers are all gone and so should be some of their protocols. Policies that are not relevant should go to the history books and not be referenced in new rulings.

2 - Disclaimer

I, the author, am not involved with prisons or prisoners but I have talked to many prisoners during Hospital Pastoral Visitations. I am sharing what is coming to me in an effort to spread understanding and trigger conversation that can be helpful. It may be that the discussion needs finessing and I invite your wisdom into the mix.

My guidance has suggested that a lot can be done. I will detail my views which are not the expert positions of a Corrections Officer or Corrections Administrator or Corrections Manager or Corrections Supervisor, or Medical Practitioner or Psychologist or Psychiatrist or Social Worker or another expert who might be helpful here.

As I have said many times before, everything that I look at about prisons seems to be so complicated. Here I reference some of my earlier books that suggested things that have come to my awareness regarding United States Sentencing Commission which appears to be making strides within a very constricted system.

Expediency could be effectuated with wholesale core issue redevelopment.

3 - Taxpayer Wish List

It is quite typical for many taxpayers to create a personal wish list when Christmas time and Spiritual Holidays occur so that their loved ones know what they would like for presents.

The Prison System could benefit from such an idea if and when taxpayers can get clear and precisely declare the changes they would like to see put to the vote for Analysis and implementation.

4 - A Precise Declaration Ready to Go

Talk is cheap and disperses in the air when the idea is not captured and polished. The idea here is to start with a precise concept, so that forward motion possibility is optimized.

First Edition of ideas must be as precise as possible so that it can get ballot-ready quickly. After an initial yes approval, a move towards development will be apparent.

Save some prisoners by defining particulars and more will follow. Helpful to consider for wishing:

1. Who?_____(a group)

2. What?_____(How)

3. Where?_____(City/Fed./State)

4. When? _____(Conditions)

5. How?._____(Program)

6. Why?_____(Justify)

5 - Where To Start

If you are reading this book, it is likely that you have areas of the system that are of particular interest to you and that would be the right place to start. Since you have that interest, it would also be good for me to caution you that your personal agenda needs to take a back seat to the process.

While this may not seem fair, the reality is that we have a complicated system and it is not geared towards adapting to the needs of individuals. The system also has a whole series of unworkable rules that were created before you were born and a rapid redirection is very unlikely.

While the last sentence may seem less fair than the earlier ones, we need to deal with all that is real. The situations in prisons may be terrible and in need of change but that will not happen quickly or easily.

Prisoners and prison system are tightly regulated, and that impedes change. Frustration and perhaps depression can come from working toward change.

Please step forward on this path by knowing that you need to bring both patience and persistence if you are to succeed. While you are not alone in wanting better times for people who you care about, the journey of pursuing change will be tedious.

You will also need to bring an organized approach which is shareable so that successes achieved will be able to benefit others long after your favorite prisoner has exited the system permanently. You need to do some research before you can start working toward specific goals.

I have published 60+ books about prison possibilities alone and offer most of them since Christmas 2017 as presents through Kindle to all who would like them. The release schedule is updated routinely on the "Prison Presents" tab of the website http://www.AngelRaphaelspeaks.com/. The direct link to get you there is http://angelraphaelspeaks.com/christmas/

Those books can offer you many ideas to pursue over time when you are ready. Before you get there, I have some ideas that could help move the whole system forward.

The book *A Million Less Prisoners Please* details a lot of ideas for reducing the number of prisoners in our facilities and other ideas to help keep free citizens out of the system.

6 - Red Tape

We the taxpayers need a way to cut through the red tape and put each critical value in a clear and unmistakable move forward format for our government representatives to act upon. We can ask our representatives at the state and local level to prep each step for voter authorization.

7 - Refined Legislation Could Cut Costs

Prisons may seem like they are "Dollar Wise & Pound Foolish (anon.)." Costs are impacted by rules, and that can make it very difficult for managers to create efficiency.

So much is regulated that it may be that administrators are just able to do as best they can with what they have. The politics of prisons may also be difficult to understand and change.

It seems that every potential change is contested and that there is no flexibility without a lot of winners and losers who need to be heard.

Consider for just a minute as if there could be a change to the legislation regarding the main rules of the system.

There is a body of people who can do that, and they are called the voters. Voters usually vote on proposals that are put forth by politicians and many times people do not vote because they feel that their votes do not matter.

Votes do matter, but the real question is who sets the legislation because they are the ones who influence the details.
The people have the power, and they can make changes when they decide to do the work that makes that happen.

Now one person may not trigger a lot of change but the dozen or so million people impacted by prison conditions towards their loved ones can when the issues are clear enough. I hope this book helps them to find and use their power.

As this book opens to discuss possibilities, please know that everybody you know who is as troubled as you can also speak to their representatives progressively more each year until things start to change. Write the proposals methodically on one key issue or many.

Details Can Put Fewer People In Jail

You will not be able to help everybody but helping others to support themselves can help many to give more and complain less.

In the next chapter, I will share a proposal again for those who wish to tell their representatives to change the sentencing which will keep a lot of people out of Jail.

After That, Additional chapters will provide more ideas for your consideration. Copy and edit what you like and ignore the rest.

Nothing here is legal advice. If you need or want a lawyer, hire one. These ideas are merely about you and millions of others writing to your representatives and asking to be represented in a way that makes you proud of their accomplishments.

It may make sense to standardize your efforts with other local citizens so that agencies consolidate their efforts. You can ask your local lawyers for suggestions.

8 - "Sentencing" (Example)
{From Chapter 11 in *A Million Less Prisoners Please*}

"The system of Jurisprudence is very complicated, and that intricate system makes progress difficult even when agencies are trying hard. The detailed system dynamics need to be unraveled, and that can be time-consuming and stressful to the whole system.

I am not proposing but suggesting that one idea to consider is merely changing the universe of prison rules by going back to the source legislation and create an authority that can supersede existing criteria.

I wrote a book called the *Answer to Sentencing*: *Help Judges Cut Minimums* that offers a discussion about a survey of judges where about fifty percent of them indicated that the mandatory minimums should be malleable at the discretion of the presiding judge. I also was aware that the 50% of the judges were roughly in alignment with an Angel Raphael message I channeled that we could cut prison costs by 47%.

My original interest was triggered by a story in the press of a Federal Judge in Nashville who quit the bench because of a job requirement that he follow the mandatory minimum rules.

My opinion is that the Judges are in the best position to know the details of each case and should have the power to choose. The voting booth is the supreme authority in this country, and all voters could vote for the highest good. I include below a form from that book that citizens could send their representatives and declare their support for Judicial discretion.

Proposed Declaration to _____

{Modified slightly from Chapter 16 of *Answer to Sentencing: Help Judges Cut Minimums*}

"We the people of _____ wish to convey to you, our esteemed representatives, that we are tremendously unhappy with the volume of our brother and sister citizens who are currently incarcerated. We feel that the laws in place are antiquated and threaten our freedom.

With all due respect, we implore you as our representatives to take on the task of fixing this problem. The social fabric of our communities needs to be protected from burdensome legal complications of the lengthy sentences created by the Mandatory Minimums.

We assert herewith the will of the people to empower the Judges to cut the sentences for non-violent offenders at the discretion of the Judges when they deem appropriate.

We would like to see the sentencing cut substantially and declare that 47% (Forty-Seven Percent) is not an unrealistic number. We would actually prefer if the average cut exceeded 22% (Twenty-Two Percent).

We trust Your diligence in compliance with our wishes."

9 - Alcoholic Program Concept

"We the people of _____ wish to convey to you, our esteemed representative, that we are tremendously unhappy with the volume of our brother and sister citizens who are currently incarcerated and have Alcohol addiction issues. We feel that the procedures in place need to be updated and provide for reasonable treatment protocols that are rehabilitative.

With all due respect, we implore you to take on the task of improving this situation. There need to be some tangible and measurable efforts to enhance the options of prisoners to rehabilitate, and we urge you to facilitate it.

We understand that funds are limited and the needs are many. We would like to see mass incarceration to shift progressively into a categorized system that focuses on the possibilities for prisoner pathways to rehabilitation.

We trust Your diligence in compliance with our wishes."

10 - Drug Addict Program Concept

"We the people of _____ wish to convey to you, our esteemed representative, that we are tremendously unhappy with the volume of our brother and sister citizens who are currently incarcerated and have Drug addiction issues. We feel that the procedures in place need to be updated and provide for reasonable treatment protocols.

With all due respect, we implore you to take on the task of improving this situation. There need to be some tangible and measurable efforts to enhance the options for prisoners to rehabilitate, and we urge you to facilitate it.

We understand that funds are limited and the needs are many. We would like to see mass incarceration to shift progressively into a categorized system that focuses on the possibilities for prisoner pathways to rehabilitation.

We trust Your diligence in compliance with our wishes."

11 - Mental Health Program Concept

"We the people of _____ wish to convey to you, our esteemed representative, that we are tremendously unhappy with the volume of our brother and sister citizens who are currently incarcerated and have Mental Health issues. We feel that the procedures in place need to be updated and provide for reasonable mental health stabilization and or treatment protocols.

With all due respect, we implore you to take on the task of evaluating and improving this situation. There need to be some tangible and measurable efforts to stabilize affected residents and enhance the options for prisoners to rehabilitate, and we urge you to facilitate them.

We understand that funds are limited and the needs are many. We would like to see mass incarceration environments shift progressively into a categorized prioritized system that focuses on the possibilities for prisoner pathways to rehabilitation.

We trust Your diligence in compliance with our wishes."

12 - Recidivism

"We the people of _____
wish to convey to you, our esteemed representative, that we are tremendously unhappy with the volume of our brother and sister citizens who are currently reincarcerated after having been discharged without having the skills to survive.

All prisoners with a reasonable expectation of freedom need to be offered preparedness information to help them be ready for the exit,

With all due respect, we implore you to take on the task of improving this situation. There need to be some tangible and measurable efforts to enhance the options for prisoners to rehabilitate, and we urge you to facilitate it.

We understand that funds are limited and the needs are many. We would like to see mass incarceration to shift progressively into a categorized system that focuses on the possibilities for prisoner pathways to rehabilitation and successful re-entry.

We trust Your diligence in compliance with our wishes."

13 - Children Need Access to Their Parents

"We the people of _____
wish to convey to you, our esteemed representative, that we are tremendously unhappy with the volume of our brother and sister citizens who are currently incarcerated and have limited or no access to their children.

With all due respect, we implore you to take on the task of improving this situation if you have any ideas on how to do it. There need to be some tangible and measurable efforts to improve the options for prisoners to be motivated to rehabilitate themselves, and we urge you to consider all possibilities.

We understand that funds are limited and the needs are many. We would like to see mass incarceration shift progressively into a categorized system that focuses on the possibilities for prisoner pathways to rehabilitation that is enhanced by connectivity with their children.

We trust Your diligence in compliance with our wishes."

14 - What Would We Vote For?

Writing laws is not easy, and everybody wants to have their say, and the government has the responsibility of dotting the "Is" and crossing the "Ts." We have the responsibility to get across what we want just like we did with the Declaration of Independence.

The Federal Government has the Senate and the House of Representatives, and they have the staff to do all the diligence that we could possibly need.

We need to convey to them what it is that we want. But do we know exactly? Probably not.

I Think We Want

To Allow Judges

To Cut Mandatory

Minimum Sentences

And Create

Additional
System Review Committees
To Make System Recommendations

15 - Political Action Plan

The Bible told us all what to do.

Ask, and it shall be given you;
seek, and ye shall find;
knock, and it shall be opened unto you:
                              Matthew 7:7

Ask for the changes that you would like to see. Seek those answers, and as you go, it shall open to you.

It is essential to be clear when asking politicians for action. I have drafted five declarations above that you can copy and use for your community if you choose.

You can also write your own. Please note that as more people say the same thing, the chances for success can increase.

The asking formats for the Federal, State, and Local levels can be edited to suit your own particular community.

Networking is Great!

Politicians in your city, village or town already have enough complainers. They are not seeking more so it would be wise to be a networker and not present yourself as one who wants to complain to your representatives.

The staff of politicians usually delight in meeting the constituents of their leaders because it is a very efficient way for them to learn how they can serve. When you share your concerns, it helps them to prepare to serve you and your neighbors.

When many people say the same thing, the politicians will get it. These same people that are trying to serve may also become your advocates, so networking might be something to consider.

If you take an interest in the community, people within it can take an interest in you and your affairs.

16 - Proposed Declaration for a City

We the people of _____
wish to convey to you, our esteemed representatives, that we are tremendously unhappy with the volume of our brother and sister citizens who are currently incarcerated. We feel that the laws in place may be somewhat antiquated and threaten the freedom of some people sometimes.

With all due respect, we implore you as our representatives to take on the task of evaluating possible steps to reduce the levels of incarceration when possible. The social fabric of our communities needs to be protected from burdensome legal complications on an ongoing basis.

We assert herewith the will of the people to empower the Judges to create reasonable options to help curtail sentences and develop creative alternatives for non-violent offenders at the discretion of the Judges when they deem appropriate.

We would like to see the sentencing minimized as much as possible. We trust your diligence in compliance with our wishes.

17 - Wrap Up

There can be great value in openness to others and a willingness to hear their views.

These ideas will not fix the incarceration problem, but they may help stabilize and reduce the level of incarceration which can maintain lower occupancy levels and help to alleviate overcrowding which itself can improve the quality of the prison experience for many.

These ideas can also help to diminish the collateral damage to children and communities who are seriously disserved by the absoluteness of current sentencing practices.

While we need to keep the communities safe, being too rigid does not help the government to provide for all the people. Common sense can be a staunch ally to rehabilitating prisoners.

While some may argue against second chances, it is evident that many prisoners will eventually reenter the community. Prisoners being ready, willing and able to survive their release and stay free productive contributors to our society will be relevant to the safety of everybody in the community.

Avoiding recidivism through first term rehabilitation and sentence truncations can go a long way to resolving mass incarceration and bringing more quality of life to the communities of America.

Family life can be enhanced through unification as early as possible.

18 - Thank You

For
Considering
These
Ideas

19 - Don't Worry Ever

It Does Not Help Prayer Still Does!

Resource: http://Create-A-Prayer.com

20 - Books Category Resources
at www.Amazon.com

Distant Healing (or Mail List) e-mail mikewann@voicenet.com

Veterans Healing Six Pack plus 2
http://angelraphaelspeaks.com/healing-books/veterans/

PTSD Power Pack
http://angelraphaelspeaks.com/healing-books/ptsd/

Angel Raphael Speaks Series & Other Angel Books
http://angelraphaelspeaks.com/

Reiki
http://angelraphaelspeaks.com/healing-books/reiki/

Children
http://angelraphaelspeaks.com/healing-books/children/

Emergency Medical Kindness
http://angelraphaelspeaks.com/healing-books/emergency-medical-kindness/

Cancer
http://angelraphaelspeaks.com/healing-books/cancer/

Addictions
http://angelraphaelspeaks.com/healing-books/addictions/

Miscellaneous Healing
http://angelraphaelspeaks.com/healing-books/misc-healing/

Prison Books - 50+ Prison Books
http://angelraphaelspeaks.com/prison-books/

21 - Angels Please Prayers

Addict's
Angels of Healing Selected
Help Me to Stay Directed
Come To Me From The Sky
I Am Ready to Succeed Not Try
If I Don't Invite You In
I Might Not Win
I Have Been Lost For Too Long
Help Me To Stay Strong

Alcoholic's
Angels of Healing On High
Help Me to Stay Dry
Come To Me From The Sky
I Am Ready to Succeed Not Try
If I Don't Invite You In
I Might Not Win
I Have Been Lost For Too Long
Help Me To Stay Strong

Prayers Above From

http://AngelRaphaelSpeaks.com/AAAAAA/
The Link Above Has the Core Messages from the book on drop-down pages.

22 - Private Channeling

Angel Raphael Speaks a series of free messages that are channeled through Reverend Mike Wanner for the Highest good and Highest Healing of all concerned.

Many questions arise about Reverend Mike doing private channeling, and he does help with that so E-mail him.

Reverend Mike is available worldwide as a psychic channel, emotional release facilitator, spiritual energy practitioner & teacher, and public speaker.

He looks forward to meeting you soon! Email - mikewann@voicenet.com 215-342-1270

PRIVATE SPIRITUAL READINGS/channelings or Spiritual Healing Sessions: Telephone or in person.

Rev. Mike is available for individual, intuitive one-on-one sessions with you, his Guide Family, and your Guides. He helps by offering clarity on emotional situations about your life, your purpose, your spirituality, and your release of stuffed emotions and cellular memory.

Connect to the love of your Guides today!

For more information, Please visit

http://angelraphaelspeaks.com/channel/

23 - Reverend Mike Wanner

Rev. Mike Wanner started his spiritual and ministerial studies with Reiki in 1993 and had studied seven styles of Reiki in the U.S., Japan, Canada, Denmark, and Australia. He is certified to teach.

He became certified to teach Integrated Energy Therapy in 1999 and co-taught the first IET class of the new Millennium. Mike began dowsing in 2001.

Ordained as an Interfaith Minister of the Circle of Miracles Ministry and a Metaphysical Minister of the International Metaphysical Ministry, Rev. Mike practices and teaches spiritual energy therapies in the Philadelphia Area.

Rev. Mike holds ministerial degrees from the University of Metaphysics and the University of Sedona. He is a Pastoral Care Associate at Jefferson - Frankford Hospital. He taught at the National Academy of Massage Therapy and Health Sciences.

Rev. Mike was a faculty member of the Medical Mission Sister's Center for Human Integration's School of Integrated Body/Mind Therapies in Fox Chase, Philadelphia, PA for twelve years.

For a complete Biography, Please visit

http://ReverendMikeWanner.com/Bio